I0161908

GROWING UP IN A LITTLE AFRICAN VILLAGE

An Illustrated Edition

GROWING UP IN A LITTLE AFRICAN VILLAGE

An Illustrated Edition

ROBERT PEPRAH-GYAMFI

Perseverance Books
Loughborough, UK

GROWING UP IN A LITTLE AFRICAN VILLAGE
An Illustrated Edition

All Rights Reserved. Copyright © 2014 Robert Peprah-Gyamfi

No part of this book may be reproduced or transmitted in any form or by any means, graphic, electronic, or mechanical, including photocopying, recording, taping or by any information storage or retrieval system, without the permission in writing from the publisher.

PERSEVERANCE BOOKS

For information address:
PERSEVERANCE BOOKS
P.O. BOX 8505
LOUGHBOROUGH
LE11 9BZ
UK
www.peprah-gyamfi.com

ISBN: 978-0-9570780-5-5

To the inhabitants of tiny Mpintimpi, the village in Ghana where my eyes first saw the light of day, past, present and future.

TABLE OF CONTENTS

-1-
THE HUMBLE BEGINNING

I GREW UP IN A SMALL VILLAGE called Mpintimpi. It is situated in the Eastern Region of Ghana, about 120 kilometres to the north of Accra, the national capital.

Today, the village has grown a little bigger. At the time I was growing up about forty years ago, however, it had only a few houses. A lorry road passed through the middle of the village from north to south to divide it into almost two equal halves. When one entered the village coming from the north, the first building on the left side of the road was our home.

It was a small rectangular mud building measuring about ten metres in length and five metres in breadth. It was about three metres high. The building had only two small rooms.

About thirty metres away from the main building, towards the bush that bordered our compound, was a smaller building, about half the size of the main building. That was our kitchen.

About ten metres behind the kitchen was a small rectangular structure. That was our bathroom. We did not have our own toilet. We used the male and female toilets at the other end of the village. Everyone in the village could use it.

-2-
THE DIFFICULT JOURNEY OF THE NEW ARRIVAL TO OUR HOME

LIKE ALMOST EVERY CHILD who was born in Mpintimpi, I was born at home. According to mother, my birth took place in the small family bathroom. It measured about one metre in length and eighty centimetres in width. The wooden wall rose to about a metre and half above ground level. At the top the structure was open to the free tropical skies. The floor was not cemented but covered with fine gravel.

By the time I was big enough to understand the world around me, we were seven children at home—five boys and two girls. I had four elder brothers and two younger sisters. In the course of time I noticed that mother's stomach was growing bigger and bigger day by day.

Soon mother began to talk about a new arrival that was expected in our home. Then one day she went into the family bathroom. Before she did so, she sent one of us to fetch Maame Gyamfuah and Maame Adwoa Adeye. These two elderly women lived near our home. Soon both women rushed into our compound.

"Where is your mother?" they asked as if with one voice. We pointed to the bathroom. Both women rushed in there. For the next several hours they remained with mother in the small bathroom. After a while, one of them came out of the small room. She looked very worried. Turning to one of my senior brothers, she began:

"Hurry up and fetch Papa Osei! Tell him we need his help quickly."

Papa Osei could be described as the village doctor. Though he never went to school, when he grew up he was good in traditional medicine and was a help to the villagers whenever they were taken ill.

It wasn't long before Papa Osei came rushing to our home and joined the women. I was too young to understand what exactly was going on. The look on the faces of the adults led me, however, to believe that all was not well with mother.

Finally, about an hour after the arrival of the 'village doctor', we could hear the screams of a baby. It was followed almost immediately by the claps and shouts of joy of the three adults attending to mother. Several minutes later, mother, who seemed to be in terrible pain, came out, assisted by the two women. Tenderly, they led her into her bedroom. She remained there for the rest of the day. My sister, mother's last child, was named Afia Serwaah.

Though several years have passed since then, I still remember that when I was very young, I had a big head and a big stomach! As a result, whenever I walked around the small settlement clothed only with a *pieto* (*pieto* is a Twi word meaning children's slip), I was made fun of not only by my peers, but also by some of the adults with calls of "bin tom,

tom!" (referring to my protruding belly) and coconut head because of my big head.

I easily lost my temper in those days, I can tell you! Needless to say, I was angered by their taunts. In my anger, I would get hold of a stone and threaten to throw it at the offender. I just could not understand why anyone would be so mean to me!

Certain worms can live inside human beings. These worms are known as parasitic worms.

A time came when my parents began to think that my big stomach was caused by worms that had found their home in my stomach! So they travelled to the next big village called Nyafoman and bought some *nsonsonaduro*, which means 'worm medicine'. On their return they gave me some of the medicine to drink. It was a green liquid and had a pleasant taste.

Mother did not leave me to empty my bowels in the public latrine as was usually the case. Instead, she gave me a chamber pot for that purpose.

I am not trying to blow up the matter! The truth is that loads of long round worms, coiled together in a large bundle, came out of my body! They looked like the large earthworms I saw on my way to farm or the riverside. Indeed, they looked very alike. Today, I know that the worms that came out of me carry the medical term *Ascaris lumbricoides* or Roundworms, which, of course, are quite different from earthworms. That they made their home in my bowels and competed with me for the very food my parents managed to put on the table was rude on their part, to say the least!

-3-
RECRUITING FOR
THE ACADEMIC JOURNEY

EVERY BOY AND GIRL IN GHANA was expected to go to school. The children in Mpintimpi faced one problem, however. Few if any of us possessed a birth certificate. "Why?" You may ask! The answer is that almost every child was born at home. Their parents did not register such births at the registry. As a result they were not issued with birth certificates.

How then could the school authorities know that we were big enough to attend school?

This is what happened. They asked all of us to get together on the veranda in front of the palace, the official residence of the chief of the village. Next, they asked each of us to use one arm to make a bow over the head and try to touch the ear on the other side of our body. Whoever was able to do so was allowed to start school.

It was common for children about to start school to adopt a 'Christian name'. Neither myself nor my older brother Kwame, who was also about to start school, had 'Christian names'. Neither father nor mother could read or write. They had also no idea of 'Christian names'. Our elder brother Ransford, who at that time was in Year 8 in the elementary school, helped to find Kwame and myself 'Christian Names'.

His method was very clever. First, he wrote down several European first names that he was aware of. Next, he asked us to listen carefully as he read them out. The rule was for us to shout "STOP!" when he called out a name that we liked. Kwame was so excited by the sound of the name 'Edmund' that he chose it for himself. For my part I selected Robert!

We had to wear a uniform. For the boys it was khaki shirts and khaki trousers. For the girls the colour of their uniform could be green, blue, pink or white, depending on the choice of the school concerned.

As we left home for school for the very first time none of the children from Mpintimpi wore a school uniform. Instead, we were clothed in our ntama. Ntama is a piece of cotton that one wears by wrapping it loosely around the body. To prevent it from slipping away from our bodies as we went through the activities of the school day, we wrapped it in such a way as to permit us to tie two ends loosely around our necks.

For a while our teachers allowed us to go to school without a uniform. A time came, though, when such pupils were sent home and not permitted to return without school uniforms.

Our parents could afford only one set of uniform. After wearing it for a year or two, it began to show signs of wear and tear. In time the small tears became bigger and bigger. Soon one could see our underwear through the torn parts of the uniform!

At the beginning, our teachers would ask us to remind our parents politely about the need to replace them. "Let's wait for the cocoa harvesting season", they would reply.

Sometimes the season passed without any sign of the 'poor uniform' being replaced. Finally the time came when the class teacher could bear the situation no longer and sent the pupil home to acquire a new uniform.

At the time I began my academic journey the school system in Ghana was made up in the main of three cycles. The first cycle, elementary school, took a minimum of six years and a maximum of ten years to complete. From there one could move on to the second cycle, secondary school. Elementary schools were spread throughout the country.

The situation was different when it came to secondary schools. They were found mainly in large towns and cities. Most of them were boarding schools. One had to leave home to stay there for about twelve weeks before returning home on holidays.

-4-
THE TEDIOUS WALK TO AND FROM SCHOOL

WE GOT UP EARLY on a typical school day. The first thing we did was to walk to the Nwi River, about a mile away to fetch water for the home. The water was collected in plastic or aluminium buckets. Each of them was able to hold between five to ten litres of water. We carried the load on our heads. On a typical day we undertook two to three trips. In the rainy season, when there was usually enough water at home, we did not have to fetch water from the Nwi River.

When there was enough time, we did have a proper bath. If there wasn't enough time and we were likely to be late getting to school, we washed only our heads, our armpits and both legs from the knee downwards. Next, we quickly ate our breakfast. It was made up usually of boiled plantains and stew. Plantain is a plant of the banana family; the plantain fruit looks like banana.

Usually all the schoolchildren from Mpintimpi walked to attend the school at Nyafoman, and did so in one single group. Those who got ready first went round the homes of the other children to ask them to hurry up. There were times when the group could not wait for everybody to get ready before starting the walk to school.

You may wonder how children as young as six years old could walk a distance of two miles to attend school. Some may also ask if there were no school buses around to carry them. No, there were no school buses, so the children had to walk.

The bigger ones among us, those in the upper classes, kept an eye on the little ones.

We walked along the main road leading to Nkawkaw. There was not much traffic on the road. Still, a few vehicles passed by as we walked along the road. The road was not tarred; beside that, it had potholes in several places. As a result, the vehicles usually travelled quite slowly. This allowed us enough time to move to the safety of the sides of the road long before the vehicles reached us.

In the dry season, the passing vehicles left considerable dust behind them. That made us very angry because we had to breathe in the dust. Beside that, it caused our uniforms to go dirty.

If the dust was a source of anger, the rain was less comforting. Yes, in the geographical region where we lived, it either rained or shined. If it rained heavily in the morning long before we set out for school, we stayed away from school for that entire day.

Usually, however, the rains did not come down early in the morning. Instead, it caught us by surprise just as we were heading for school, or returning home from school. In such situations, we were left with no other choice than to take an involuntary shower, for hardly any of us carried an umbrella. If by chance one of us was carrying a cutlass (a blade with a handle that we used to weed on our plots—I will tell you more about our plots later), we cut the broad leaves of a banana or plantain tree growing in the farms bordering the road and used them as a kind of umbrella.

Sometimes the problems brought by the rain were made worse by the vehicles travelling on the road! As I just told you, there were potholes on the road. When it rained, 'ponds' of water gathered in several places on the road, so when the passing vehicles drove through them, they sent splashes of dirty water in all directions to soil our clothes.

We thought that some of the drivers just wanted to show off—yes, to let us know that they were the masters of the road! Why did we think that way?! Sometimes they seemed to drive through ponds of water on the road that we thought they could have easily avoided!

Even if the vehicle passing by on a rainy day did not cause us problems, the mud caused by the rain did so by soiling our feet. Fortunately, there was a small stream a few hundred metres away from school so we went there and cleaned our feet before reaching the school compound.

The fact that all of us walked barefoot to school brought us another problem. In Africa it can be very hot. The hot sun caused the ground we were walking on to be heated. As we walked along the hot ground we could feel the burning under the soles of our feet!

On some occasions, the driver of a vehicle pulled over and gave us a lift! That did not happen very often, however. In the first place, most of the vehicles that passed by were already filled to the last seat. Even if a vehicle had a few seats left, the fact that we usually walked in a group of no less than six pupils at a time might have caused the driver to decide not to stop. Just think about it—if the driver stopped and did not have a seat for everybody, what would he do? Should he take only some of us and leave the rest? What would the others think? To avoid such an awkward situation the driver probably chose to drive on and not stop!

-5-
FLIES AND BEES DISTURBING THE MORNING ASSEMBLY

W E REALLY HAD TO HURRY UP to avoid being late for school, for being late for school could lead to trouble. What kind of trouble, you ask? Well, one could be punished for arriving late. Later I will write about the forms of punishment one could expect!

One had to be at school several minutes before the beginning of lessons. Why the need to do so? The reason was that schoolchildren were responsible for tidying the classrooms as well as the compound surrounding the school.

The whole school population was divided into four sections. The names of the sections were Blue, Green, Red and Yellow. Each section had a leader selected from a pupil in the most senior class; in the case of the primary school this was primary class 6. Each section also had a teacher to supervise it.

The school compound was divided among the four sections. The section in turn gave each pupil a piece of plot. It was our duty to keep our portion of plot tidy, including weeding it and also collecting any trash that might have fallen on it.

It was expected that every pupil would visit their plot every day to make sure it was tidy. At regular intervals the section teacher, or sometimes the head teacher himself, went round to inspect the plots. Such inspections were mostly unannounced! Each pupil had to stand on their plot during the inspection. The pupil whose plot was found to be untidy could be caned!

The actual school day began at 8:30 a.m. with an assembly that was held in the open, in front of the school building. Each class lined up in two parallel lines facing the school building, short girls in the very front followed by the tall ones; then the short boys like myself, and finally the tall ones at the rear.

Even the way in which we formed the lines could bring a pupil into trouble. The lines were expected to be straight, and anyone caught disrupting the line could be called forward and caned before the whole school. To form a nice straight line each of us stretched out their right arm and touched the shoulder of the child in front of them. After the school prefect or the pupil on duty that day was satisfied the line was straight and neat, we were told to put our hands down.

The assembly was opened with a short Christian prayer. Though it was a state school, that fact did not cause offence to anyone. The population of the area was mostly Christian, the remaining being believers in various traditional African forms of worship. At that period about twenty per cent of the population of Ghana were Muslims. Most Muslims lived in northern Ghana, several miles away from our little village.

The prayer was followed by the recitation of the national pledge. Yes, every child was expected to recite a short passage. In it we promised to love our country Ghana and to do all we could to keep the good name of the country. Every pupil had to stand in the 'Salute Position' during the recitation.

Next, we sang the first stanza of the national anthem, which begins with "God Bless our Homeland Ghana". Each one of us was required to stand in the 'attention' position during the singing of the anthem. In our part of the world, one can easily be disturbed by a fly or a bee, or both. Even if that happened as we sang the anthem, we were still required not to move! Those who were caught moving could expect some lashes from a cane as soon as the song was over.

After the pledge and the national anthem came the announcements for the day. These were read either by the teacher on duty, or the head teacher. Finally, we marched into our classrooms. As we did so we sang a song, what we called a marching song.

The school day was divided into two main sessions, namely the morning and the afternoon. For the primary school, which could be described as Years 1 to 6 of the elementary school, the morning session began at 8:30 a.m. and ended at 11:30 a.m. This was followed by a lunch break which lasted until 1.30 p.m. The afternoon session ended at 3.30 p.m.

In the case of the middle school (Years 7 to Year 10) the morning session was from 8:30 a.m. to 12:00 noon followed by a lunch break, which lasted until 1:30 p.m. In their case, the evening session ended at 4:00 p.m.

In the primary school one particular exercise was repeated almost every morning. This was commonly known as 'mental'. During 'mental' we were given problems in arithmetic, usually ten, sometimes twenty, to solve. We had to find the answer mentally. That means we were not allowed to first write them down. The teacher usually found the time to mark it soon after it was over. One or two mistakes by a pupil were usually permitted. More errors could result in the pupil being caned.

During the lunch break, our classmates who lived in Nyafoman returned home to enjoy hot meals prepared by their parents or relatives or, in some cases, by themselves.

Pupils like me who did not come from Nyafoman had two choices as far as the afternoon meal was concerned. First, they could bring already cooked meals along in the morning to be eaten during the break. Second, they could carry uncooked foodstuffs with them and cook them during the break time. The second option was favoured by those who happened to have relations or friends who lived nearby and were prepared to allow them into their homes to prepare their meals there.

Yes, we had to cook the food on our own, because our parents were back in Mpintimpi.

As I mentioned earlier, we usually did mental arithmetic every morning. Dictation was popular in the afternoon. In that case, the teacher read out ten to twenty words that had to be spelt correctly. As in the case of 'mental', those who scored below the accepted mark set by the teacher could be caned.

-6-
THE YOUNG ACADEMIC
ON THE POINT OF EXPLOSION

WALKING HOME FROM SCHOOL in the evening was even more tedious compared to the morning walk to school. I was not only tired from the day's work at school, I was usually also hungry and thirsty.

Do not think that we could straightaway rest on returning home after a long day at school! No, our parents expected us to help them at home, especially to help them prepare the evening meal.

Fufu was and still is our main evening meal. The food items have to be pounded for some time into balls in a wooden mortar with the help of a wooden pestle. The balls are then swallowed down with soup. Our parents expected us to help pound the *fufu*. The pounding of *fufu* can take between half an hour and an hour. It was hard work and one could sweat a lot when pounding *fufu*!

Just think about it—you have walked to school, taken part in the school activities of the day, walked back home, only to be called upon to pound *fufu*! But don't blame our parents! They themselves would until then also have worked hard the whole day, in their case in the tropical heat, both on the farm and at home.

As I mentioned earlier, we did not have electricity. It could be very dark at night. Usually our teachers gave us homework that needed to be completed before the next day, so we had to resort to kerosene lanterns or Swiss kerosene lamps to provide the light for us to read and write. This meant we had to endure the hot blasts of heat that came from the kerosene lamps!

It was no fun learning with those lamps or lanterns, believe me! The smell of the burning fuel was, to put it mildly, irritating. While the 'young academic' was already struggling with an assignment, the smell of the burning fuel added insult to injury—or you could say rubbed salt into the wound! Under such circumstances, any perceived provocation from one or other resident of the home— laughter, a scream, or a shout—could cause the aspiring academic to almost explode with fury.

We retired to bed around 9 p.m. "Good night and sleep well!" you might want to wish us. That was indeed well deserved—if only the mosquitoes were of the same mind! But no! Instead, they came to feed on us. One could somehow understand this, for it was our blood that provided them with their dinner. If only they would quietly suck our blood and leave us to sleep! But no, they disturbed our sleep, first by means of the hissing noise they made and also by means of the burning and itching sensation caused by their stings.

-7-
THE AWFUL EXPERIENCE WITH THE RED-HOT IRON

W E TRIED TO WASH OUR SCHOOL UNIFORMS on returning home from the farm on Saturdays. In case we failed to do so on Saturday, we did it the next day, Sunday.

During the dry season, when water was difficult to come by at home, we carried our dirty items to the Nwi River to get them washed there. During the rainy season, when there was a regular supply of rainwater to fill our water-collecting containers, we did the washing at home. After washing our clothes with our hands, we left them hanging in the sun to dry.

Our parents were so busy working on the farm and at home that they hardly had time to help us with the ironing of our school uniform. In the end we were left with no choice than to do so ourselves. Sometimes, the elder brothers and sisters helped their younger ones perform the task. That was not always the case, however. Sometimes the older brothers and sisters felt disrespected by their naughty junior ones and left them to sort out their own affairs.

We did not press, or iron, our uniforms on tables. Instead, we spread bed sheets on the bare cement floor of our room, and ironed our clothes on that. We had to kneel beside the sheet to be able to do so.

I still remember an awful experience I had one day as I was pressing my school uniform. I was barely ten years old at the time. As I knelt beside the bed sheet spread on the floor while moving the red-hot iron to and fro on the uniform, the hot iron tilted. This caused me to lose my balance. Before I could prevent it, the top part of my right thigh came into direct contact with the hot metal!

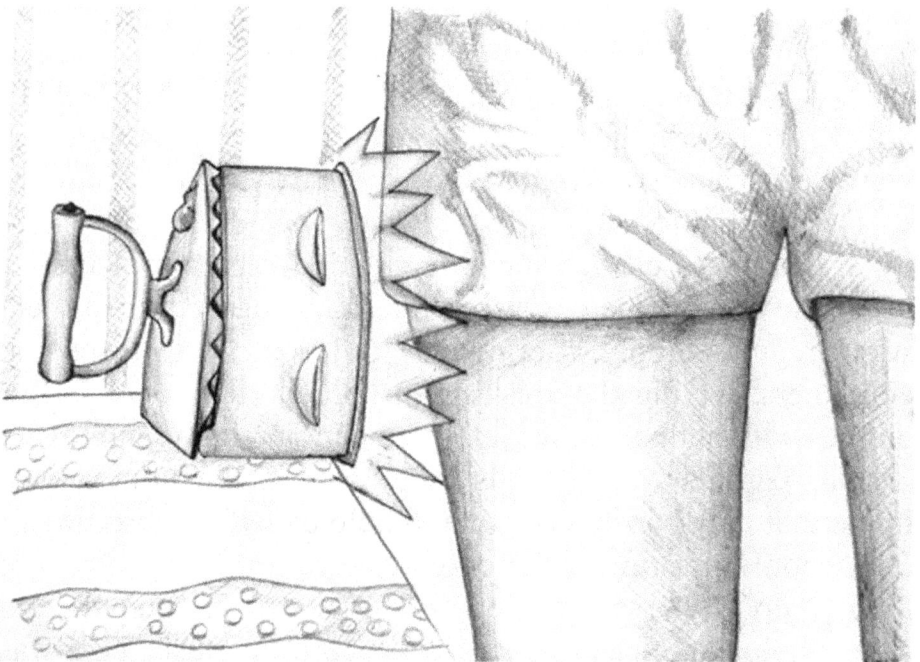

"O-o-o-h!" I screamed at the top of my voice. Everyone at home rushed to find out what was wrong with me.

"O-o-o-h! O-o-o-h! O-o-o-h!" I kept on screaming.

The rest of the family tried to comfort me, but no, I was inconsolable as I kept on screaming and yelling at the top of my voice! It really did hurt, for the metal burnt away a chunk of skin, the shape of a triangle measuring about five centimetres at the base and narrowing to about four centimetres on each side.

Did my parents take me to see the doctor? No, they didn't. As you will learn later, the nearest hospital was at Nkawkaw, about thirty kilometres away. Indeed, apart from pouring some cold water on the wound to cool it, nothing else was done.

A saying in Twi, my mother tongue, has it that God helps drive away insects from the animal that does not have a tail. My parents, in line with that thinking, might have trusted Divine grace to help sort the matter out. And so it happened, for the wound soon healed on its own without any problems.

-8-
THE CALL TO DISCIPLINE
AND THE NEED TO IMPROVISE

RESIDENTS OF MPINTIMPI were poor peasants. Many of them did not have enough money to spend on their children's education. The Government did what it could to help. One way of helping them was to supply free textbooks as well as exercise books. There were a few areas such as teaching aids where parents were expected to supply the requirements for their own children.

Although we could probably have purchased them in the big towns, counters for arithmetic lessons were made by each child, either on their own or with the help of the child's parents. To make counters, we cut branches of some of the trees growing in our area and hewed out fifty or a hundred pieces, as the case may be. These we tied together with plastic or cotton threads. Alternatively, we resorted to picking wild berries growing in the area that could serve as beads. Each of us collected fifty or a hundred, dividing them into small sacks, and took them along to the arithmetic class.

Each pupil was expected to display a high standard of discipline or else risk being punished. Punishment for the boys was usually in the form of lashes to the palm or the buttocks. Girls, however, were usually spared being caned on the buttocks. Instead, they normally received their lashes on their palms.

One could be caned for various reasons, including the following:

- Failure to keep to the personal standards of hygiene expected of each pupil—keeping fingernails cut, keeping teeth clean, keeping hair short and combed, keeping the school uniform tidy and nicely pressed.
- Failure to keep the plot assigned to him/her tidy.
- Failure to get the homework done in proper time.
- Failure to score well in mental arithmetic or dictation.
- Chatting in class in the presence or absence of the class teacher.

Yes, we were expected to be silent even when our class teachers were not around. The responsibility fell on the class captain, sometimes selected solely by the class teacher, sometimes elected by the whole class through secret ballot, to ensure that order was maintained in the class. Failure on their part to do so could lead to them being punished. To prevent that kind of situation, they usually wrote down the names of those who disturbed the silence during the absence of the teacher, to be submitted when called upon to do so.

Sometimes a pupil who did something wrong was not caned. Instead the pupil was made to write a sentence several times. These are examples of the sentences one could be asked to write:

I WILL ALWAYS BE PUNCTUAL FOR CLASS
I WILL NO LONGER DISTURB THE CLASS
I WON'T BE RUDE TO MY TEACHER, etc.

One could also be made to weed a portion of the school compound.

-9-
CALL IT CHILD LABOUR
IF YOU WILL!

DURING OUR SCHOOLDAYS, our teachers used us to perform several kinds of jobs. The jobs varied, depending on whether it involved primary or middle school pupils. We could for example be used to help a farmer harvest maize. There were two aspects of this. It could be that the farmer had done the harvesting on his own, and our duty was to carry the harvested maize in baskets back home. On certain occasions we did the harvesting as well as transporting the produce to the home of the farmer involved.

Rarely could a farmer provide enough baskets for every child. Usually an announcement was made on the day prior to carrying out the job, calling on every pupil to carry a basket or a tray to school. The very young among us, especially those in primary years 1 to 3, were usually exempt from this type of work. If such a job needed to be done, it was usually carried out during the afternoon session; the morning session on the other hand was rarely used for non-academic activity.

It was not uncommon for the schoolchildren to be called upon to fetch water to fill the water containers of their teachers—or the wives and in some cases the concubines of their teachers. As might be expected, that job was performed mostly in the dry season. We usually collected the water either from wells or the Nwi River, which served Nyafoman also.

One particular job we did was not free from danger, namely the cutting of bamboo sticks. The sticks grew widely in the woods around Nyafoman. The bamboo sticks were used in various ways—to build fences or hedges around the school garden to prevent sheep and goats from destroying the crops, or for constructing raised structures to dry cocoa beans, in buildings, etc.

Due to the danger associated with the cutting we were usually accompanied by part of the teaching staff who selected those they considered mature enough for the assignment to do the cutting. Other children were left with the duty of carrying the sticks on their heads over a distance of about a mile or more back to school. Because the bamboo stick could attain considerable heights, it could hardly be carried by a single pupil. Instead, two pupils, one at the head, the other at the tail, were made to carry a single stick back to school.

One might want to know what kind of hazard was posed by the bamboo sticks that we cut. The main one involved the cutting itself. We did so with the help of machetes. Sometimes after one had cut through about half of the stem, it broke with such force that the stick forcefully sprang into the air. In such a situation, one stood in danger of being pierced in the foot, leg or even in the body! Though I did not personally witness any of us getting injured on such assignments, reports of cases of schoolchildren elsewhere getting hurt, in some cases seriously, by bamboo sticks made their rounds from time to time.

What happened to the money earned by the school as a result of such activities? Well, our teachers never tired of reminding us, especially when a job was in hand, that the money earned was meant for the good of the school— to be used for the purchase of footballs and jerseys for the school team, the acquisition of medication and other material for the first-aid box. It also contributed towards the end of year school feast.

-10-
THE SCHOOL FEAST AND
THE TERMINAL REPORT

A SCHOOL FEAST to mark the end of a term was 'our day'. The common practice was for each class to organise a feast to mark the end of the first and second terms. The feast for the end of the third term, the academic year, on its part usually involved the whole school.

When the feast was organised by a class, the teacher asked pupils to bring their share of food from home. One had the option to enjoy it alone or share it with one's friends. The latter was usually the case. Usually friends joined their tables and enjoyed their meals together, eating from the same dish. It was an advantage on such occasions to have friends whose parents were well-to-do, who could afford to prepare rich meals that one's own parents could not afford.

At the end of the school year, many schools invested part of the money earned during the academic year performing various jobs to throw a party for the whole school population. Depending on how much money the school could afford, a sheep or a goat or several fowl were acquired for the purpose. Usually rice and yams went with a tasty sauce.

Before we were dismissed home for each holiday, our teachers handed out our terminal reports. This was not done confidentially or privately, on an individual basis, but rather before the whole class. That happened at the end of the first and second terms. At the end of the third term, the ritual took place before an assembly of the whole school.

Whatever the setting, the ritual followed a similar pattern. The class teacher stood in front of the class or the school and, beginning from the pupil who attained the overall best mark in all the subjects downwards, they called out the names of the class. At the call of each name, the pupil concerned stepped forward to collect their terminal report. The accompanying applause grew less intense until it ceased altogether by the time it was the turn of the fifth or sixth pupil.

One might imagine the expression on the faces of fellow classmates, as name after name followed and they failed to hear their names! The tension was particularly high during the end of year gathering, when a pupil might realise for the first time that they would have to repeat the class. When the news finally came home to such pupils, some of them broke down in tears; for a while some were inconsolable. It was a pathetic sight to behold.

-11-
MY COUSIN THE DRIVER

OUR PARENTS did not have the money to buy us toys, so we made them ourselves. Among other things we built our own cars. My cousin, Kwaku Driver, had a particular interest in cars and built them on his own. Because he was very fond of cars we gave him the nickname 'Driver'.

Kwaku designed and built his own toy cars making use of the fibre from the branches of the raffia palm. The raffia palm is a type of plant that grows in our part of the world.

Kwaku was able to build models of Bedford trucks, Mercedes Benz buses, Toyota pick-ups, etc. This is how he went about it. First he built the body of the vehicle involved using the branches of the raffia palm. That was not the end of the story. He needed to fit tyres onto his toy cars. How did he solve the problem? Well, the *Onyina* tree provided the answer. *Onyina* is a tree that grows in our part of the world. The roots of the young tree are evenly round in circumference. That made it suitable for use as tyres.

So when we wanted to fit tyres to our self-made toy cars, we left for the woods, dug around the roots of an *Onyina* tree and lay them bare of soil. Next we cut out a root and carried it home. On reaching home we cut out our 'tyres' from it and fitted them to our 'vehicles'. It was real fun pushing our brand new vehicles around.

-12-
THE TREACHERY OF
THE FARMER'S KIDS EXPOSED

THEN, AS NOW, THE RESIDENTS of Mpintimpi engaged in subsistence farming.

Just as in the case of my father, everybody who lived at Mpintimpi was a farmer. We did not have machines such as tractors and water-spraying equipment to help us. We had to clear the bush on our own. Not only that, we also had to fell the big trees on our own. Father did so using an axe.

I could only wonder how father was able to fell some of the large trees growing on some of our fields. At times it took him a whole day of hard work to fell one large tree. There were times when he could not fell a tree on a single day. He had to return to continue the next day.

To be able to plant crops on the field we burnt the bushes that had been cleared. After the field had been cleared and the bush burnt, we began to sow crops on the field. We had to help our parents plant the crops. Among the crops we planted were cocoa, maize, banana, tomatoes and pepper.

As I just mentioned, we, the children, had to help plant the crops. In the case of maize, we placed the seeds in our pocket and went about the field to plant them. First we dug a shallow hole with our pointed machetes. Next, we placed three to four seeds into the hole before covering them with soil. We then moved a step or two forward and did the same again.

Our parents trusted us to do a good job. That is what we usually did. At times, however, towards the end of the day, we got very tired. At that time we were tempted and thought of a quicker way of getting rid of the grains of maize still in our pockets. What did we do?

We began to fill each hole with far more seeds than our parents had asked us to do.

It did not take long for our parents to find out, however! Maize and cocoa seeds only need a few days to germinate. From time to time our parents went round the field to check and see if everything was in order. When they found several maize or cocoa seedling springing up from the same hole, they became angry.

"Who amongst you committed such treachery?!" As might be expected, each of us kept quiet. They had no choice but to go round removing the surplus seedlings.

A few weeks after we had finished planting the crops, we had to weed the farm. If we failed to do that, the crops would not grow well because the weeds would compete with them for nutrients and sunshine. In this case, also, we, the children, had to help our parents.

Finally, we had to harvest the crops that we had planted. As I mentioned earlier, we did not have machines to help us. We had to do everything ourselves. Let us take maize as an example. Our parents first cut the plant, and then the cob from the plant. It was our duty to gather the cobs into baskets and carry them to a central collecting point on the farm.

Whenever we were returning home from the farm, we had to carry loads home. As in almost every aspect of daily activity in the village, we, the children, had in this instance also to help carry the items home. Thus, after several hours of hard work on the farm, the farmer's child returned home late in the afternoon with his parents bearing some of the load on their head. The situation was not made easier by the scorching African sun or the torrential rains that could set in to pound them mercilessly as they walked home, their necks almost breaking under the heavy load.

-13-
GROWING COCOA FOR
THE CHOCOLATE FACTORY

C OCOA GROWS WELL IN GHANA. Indeed, Ghana is one of the leading producers of the crop. The products obtained from cocoa include chocolate, cocoa cake and cocoa drink.

Mpintimpi is located in the geographical area in Ghana where cocoa is grown. My parents had a few cocoa farms. They relied on the money earned from the sale of cocoa to support the whole family.

The cocoa seeds are found in pods. Each pod may contain twenty to sixty seeds or beans. (The seed of the cocoa fruit are also called beans.)

When they are not ripe, the pods are green in colour. Later they turn from green to yellow. That is the time when they are ripe enough to be harvested. A cocoa farm filled with trees, each carrying several ripe yellow pods ready to be harvested, is a beautiful scene to behold. The pods are harvested from the trunk or branches as the case may be with machetes or implements specially made for the purpose.

Harvesting is done by adults, usually men. Children, from the age of about ten onwards, followed the adults as they harvested the beautiful golden pods from the trees and gathered them into heaps, each consisting of about a dozen pods.

As a next step, the small heaps of cocoa pods were carried to a single point on the farm. Do I need to repeat the fact that children helped do this job as well?

After all the pods had been collected at a single point on the farm, they were cut open with the help of a machete. That was usually done by the adults. The beans found in the pod were emptied into a basket. Children big enough for the job helped to free the cocoa beans from the pulp surrounding it.

The beans obtained from the pods were gathered together into a heap and covered with the broad leaves of the banana plant. The heap was left on the farm for about a week. This was necessary to help give the beans the required taste.

After this, the beans were carried home and dried in the sun for about two weeks. Finally, the beans were ready to be sold.

-14-
NO DOCTOR TO TREAT
THE SICK OF MPINTIMPI

WHEN SOMEONE FALLS SICK, the first thought that normally comes to mind is to consult a doctor. This was not the case with the inhabitants of Mpintimpi.

Several factors accounted for this.

The nearest hospital is situated at Nkawkaw, which, as I mentioned earlier, is about thirty kilometres away.

Many of the inhabitants did not have the money needed to pay the transport fare.

Secondly, only a few vehicles passed through the village during the whole day.

In the third place, by the time the vehicles reached the village there were only a few or no seats left in or on them.

Finally, the inhabitants were poor farmers. Usually, when they fell sick, they had not enough money to pay the transport fare to the hospital as well as the hospital charges.

So, usually when we fell sick my parents collected herbs from the woods, boiled them and gave us the resulting liquid to drink. Sometimes they used part of the liquid obtained from boiling the leaves to wash us. They did not use just any type of leaves. No, they used leaves from plants that were known to be able to cure diseases.

If this method did not help and the person was still feeling very ill, their family borrowed money from neighbours who could help and took the sick person to hospital.

-15-
THE THIEF THAT STRIKES FROM ABOVE

WE RAISED LIVESTOCK at home, not on a large scale, but mainly for our own use. We were not very successful in our efforts to raise poultry. Several factors accounted for this.

In the first place, we did not feed them as well as we should. We had no idea of the poultry feeds we should have purchased in the big towns for our birds to feed on. Even if we did we would not have been able to afford them. We could have fed them on the maize we produced on our own. Well, we badly needed the money we obtained from selling our maize so were not keen to feed our birds on it.

Then there was the danger posed by traffic. A road passed through our little village to divide it into two almost equal halves. Though the road was not very busy with traffic, still enough vehicles passed on it to pose a danger to our birds. Why then, you ask, didn't we keep them in chicken houses or coops? Indeed, we had a small house for poultry. The general practice in the village, however, was to allow the chickens to roam about freely during the day. They only went back to the coop to rest at night.

Sadly, some of our birds were run over by passing vehicles. On some of these occasions the poor birds were crushed to pieces, making it impossible for us to make any use of their flesh.

On other occasions, the vehicle did not cause much damage to the body of the dead bird. In that case we picked it up from the street and made a delicious chicken soup with it. Though I was sad because of what had happened to our bird, the opportunity to enjoy chicken meat gladdened my heart! As I will write later in the book, enjoying chicken meat was usually reserved for special occasions, such as Christmas and Easter.

Our birds faced danger that came not only on land, but also from the air. Our area abounded with crows that hunted our birds from above. The crows were a danger to our birds. They would, as if from nowhere, appear in the sky, make a forceful dive downwards towards their prey, grasp the poor bird in its claws and fly away just as swiftly as they arrived. The hunting expedition of the 'thief' from the air was carried out so briskly and with such precision, it left the human inhabitants hardly any time for counter attack.

The most serious threat to our birds came, however, in the form of diseases that threatened to kill our entire livestock. At home we did not consume the birds that fell seriously ill, or indeed that dropped dead. However, someone's poison is another man's breakfast, as the saying goes, for there were a few residents amongst us who enjoyed the birds whether seriously ill or dead as a result of a disease! For such individuals, the outbreak of diseases among our birds ushered in a period of almost daily feasting on chicken meat.

It was very sad indeed to lose almost the entire stock of birds after spending so much energy and time to raise them. There was no veterinary centre around where we could send our birds for treatment. Even if there were any, we would not have had the money to pay for their treatment.

-16-
OUR STUBBORN FOUR-LEGGED COMPANIONS

SEVERAL HOUSEHOLDS in the settlement kept goats and sheep on a small scale. Hardly any of us kept them locked in barns during the day. Some keepers did not even have barns at all where the animals could be retired to sleep at night. Instead, the animals were left to sleep under the veranda or under trees within the compound. The general practice was to allow animals to roam about in the settlement during the day. The animals seemed intelligent enough to return home on their own at the onset of darkness.

The sheep, generally, were easy to keep. Not so the goats! Goats are indeed stubborn creatures. Our goats, it seemed, simply did not respect or fear us! By their behaviour they often created the impression of having fun in provoking the human beings around into anger.

You could spot them attempting to do something silly. You shouted at them to express your displeasure. At first they would pretend they did not hear you, taking no notice of you, but would stop their bad behaviour if you kept on shouting. However, the moment you turned your attention to something else they would return to what they were doing and continue to commit the same offence—if not worse.

There were instances when they set their sights on a chunk of food a human being was just enjoying. By the time one became aware of their interest, they had already grasped it and were running away with it!

One did not only have one's stubborn goats to contend with; those belonging to the immediate or even distant neighbour would come around to cause trouble as well.

-17-
MY UNCLE,
THE PROFESSIONAL HUNTER

FATHER DID ALL HE COULD to support his family, including hunting for wildlife or bush meat. He managed to acquire, under permission from the local government authority, a single-barrelled shotgun for this purpose. Because he had a lot of work to do on his farm and also at home, he hardly found the time to go hunting.

The situation was different for my uncle, Kofi Ntrama. One might as well describe him as a professional hunter. He went hunting on a regular basis. Rarely did Kofi Ntrama return from a hunting expedition empty-handed. Among some of the prey he hunted were antelopes, grasscutters, and squirrels.

-18-

THE EXPERT GRASSCUTTERS AND THE RATS FROM GAMBIA

FROM TIME TO TIME, we undertook an expedition to hunt for grasscutters. Another name for the grasscutter is the greater cane rat.

The grasscutter has rounded ears, a short nose, and coarse, bristly hair. They feed on grasses and cane; they also have a taste for cultivated foods, in particular maize and sugar cane.

It is their taste for cultivated maize that brought them in conflict with the human inhabitants. We would plant our maize or rice or cassava with much sweat, only to visit our farms in the morning to find that the cane rats had partied on our precious crops during the night!

We went after them assisted by our dogs. Indeed, without our dogs we would hardly have been able to hunt them, for not only were they quicker than ourselves, they usually hid themselves under a dense growth of bushes we could reach only with great difficulty or not at all.

On certain Saturdays, and also during the school holidays, after we had completed work on the farm, one of us would come up with the idea to go hunting for the Gambian pouched rat.

Also known as the African giant pouched rat, this rodent lives commonly in hillocks and termite mounds. The Gambian pouched rat is omnivorous, feeding on vegetables, insects, palm fruits, etc. They hide in their homes during the day and at night venture out under the cover of darkness to look for food.

When we arrived at a hillock or mound, we looked for signs of occupation by the four-legged beings we were seeking. These included fresh claw marks left on passages and alleys leading into the heart of the hillock or mound.

Next, we looked out for all possible openings leading into the heart of the hillock or mound that might serve as an escape route for the animal we were after. With the help of the branches of trees growing in the area we blocked some of the openings. Some of us would then take our positions beside a few openings that we decided to leave open.

If, as was usually the case, a dog (or a few dogs) accompanied us, it, or they, too, were made to guard some of the possible escape routes.

As a next step, we cut a long stalk from the surrounding bush. We inserted it deep into one of the openings of the mound and began to move it to and fro, so as to disturb the peace of the rat we thought was living there and force it into the open.

Some appeared from their homes minutes later. We were then either able to hunt them or they managed to escape. We would not leave them to escape without a chase, however. With the help of our dogs we were always in hot pursuit. Sometimes we were able to catch them; in other cases, we missed them.

What happened if, in spite our efforts to force them into the open, they remained stubborn and refused to come out? If the signs that led us to believe the hillock was inhabited were not very strong, we gave up after a while and went on our way.

If, on the other hand, we were still sure that it was inhabited, we took a step further in our attempt to force the rat to come out of its hiding place. We gathered dried leaves that had fallen from plants growing in the area, heaped them at one of the entrances to the mound, and set fire to them. Making use of a fan we had ourselves built using the branches of the oil palm tree (the trees could be found almost everywhere), one of us fanned the fire. This was done not only to keep the fire burning but also to help spread the smoke into the heart of the hillock. Soon smoke could be seen coming from all the openings to the burrow, including those which until then we had not discovered.

Usually it took a few minutes of fanning to force the rats into the open. If they failed to appear after a while we decided either to abandon our efforts or go a further step by cutting the hillock open! We did not attempt to cut every such mould open. Indeed, it was only when the hillock was small and we were quite sure it was occupied that we went that far.

Sometimes we would shed much sweat digging into the belly of the hillock, only to find no trace of the animal we were pursuing. Had it already escaped? Had we deceived ourselves into thinking the mound was occupied? In other instances we found the animal already dead! Deprived of oxygen, it could no longer live.

-19-
THE BITING SCISSORS AND
THE CRAWLING BEINGS

HUNTING FOR CRABS was a real adventure! The crabs found in our area lived in burrows in swampy areas bordering on ponds, streams and small rivers. Usually such burrows were partly filled with water that hid their occupants. On rare occasions one might meet them in the open during the daytime.

How were we sure a hole found in a swampy area that was partly filled with water was occupied by a crab? The answer is that they usually left their fresh 'footprints' at the entrance to their hiding places!

After we had satisfied ourselves that a particular hole was occupied by a crab, we set about hunting it. Kneeling beside the hole, we slowly and carefully extended our hand far below the water level. One had to be careful the moment one's fingers began to go under the surface of the water, for one could at any moment find one's hand very close to the crab—confirmed by a sharp stab of pain! Hardly anyone would allow a stranger into their home without putting up a fight.

Well, that was exactly what the crabs did! The moment they detected the approach of our fingers they put up a challenge!

The crabs we hunted had five pairs of claws with which they moved about. The first of each set of claws is prominent. Not only are they large, each is shaped like a pair of scissors. The crabs used the two big claws to defend themselves from the human intruders. Despite their fierce response, an experienced catcher could still hunt them without sustaining a 'bite'.

That was not always the case, however. Sometimes, though one was very careful in one's attempt to catch them, one got one or more of one's fingers trapped in one or even both of the scissor-like claws. When that happened, the crab usually bit hard! Soon one could hear the screams or yells of the unfortunate victim! On some occasions, the crab bit so hard, it led to a cut wound. Despite the possibility of being bitten by them, we hunted the crabs on a regular basis, particularly during the rainy season when one could be sure of a good catch.

On other occasions we went in search of land snails. Two kinds of land snail are found in the woods surrounding Mpintimpi; one dwells only on the ground, whereas the other does not live only on land but can be found crawling on small and medium-sized trees growing in the area.

Though one might come across them at any time of the year, the main season for snails was the rainy season. During the rainy season we went into the woods to look for the crawling creatures. Usually they hid under leaves shed by the trees growing in the area. With the help of our cutlasses we turned the fallen leaves over at places where we thought the snails could be hiding.

At certain times the snails appeared in abundance. On such occasions, a resident of the village who was known for inventing wild stories began to tell us children that he came across snails that had 'rained' down from the skies with the rains!

Going in search of snails could be risky. The crawling creatures usually lived in moist and swampy areas. This turned out to be the kind of area in which a creature we could not call our friend, namely, the python, also liked to live!

Not only did pythons live in the damp area where the snails could be found, they, like the snails, also hid themselves under fallen leaves. On some occasions one of us would turn over a heap of leaves hoping to find a snail only to discover, instead, a python! One can imagine our reaction at that moment—we took to our heels and fled as fast as our legs could carry us!

The python can be described as a lazy creature. Indeed we have a saying in Twi that goes like this: "As lazy as the python." Indeed, sometimes, after the initial shock, one or two of us gathered the courage to return to the scene to attempt to kill the serpent. Often we saw it in the same position we had initially found it—fast asleep! We then cut a long thick stick and destroyed it from a safe distance.

-20-
BE ON THE WATCH OUT FOR THE ANGRY SNAKES!

W E SET TRAPS on land, in rivers and streams.
We laid two types of traps on land. The first type was laid in a random manner in the woods to catch an animal roaming in the forest. The second type was targeted at animals such as grasscutters and rats that fed on our crops.

The traps were inspected on a regular basis, usually every other day. Whoever goes to inspect a trap needs to approach the trap with extreme caution, for it could happen that instead of finding the animal one was looking for—a grasscutter, a rat or a squirrel—in the trap, one could meet a snake that was still alive and very angry!

The traps we laid in the Nwi River were specially woven from the branches of either the raffia or oil palm tree. Several of the traps were lined up at the same spot across the river. To prevent them from being carried away by the current, we supported them with structures we built across the stream. These traps, like those set on land, were also usually inspected every other day.

-21-
ORDINARY AND EXTRAORDINARY FISHING METHODS

O N SOME OCCASIONS some of us fished in the Nwi River. We bought the hooks and lines from the weekly market at Nyafoman. We used earthworms we found along the riverbank as bait. I was not particularly keen on undertaking such ventures for the catch was usually scant. With some luck, several hours of effort might be rewarded with some tilapia or eels, or both.

Another method we used to catch fish from the streams found in our area was known locally as *ahweye*. This method involved building a dam across two sections of a stream, at a distance of about twenty metres from each other and draining the section of the river trapped by both dams almost dry of water and catching any fish found in the area. Finally, both dams were broken to restore the flow of the stream or river.

The dry season was a favourable time of the year to undertake such expeditions. The lack of rainfall would have already led several sections of the stream to be almost completely (if not completely) cut off from the main stream, permitting us to empty them without the need to first dam them.

Mother was particularly fond of undertaking *ahweye* expeditions. Although not all her children shared her interest, we usually joined her—after all, she had not only her interest at heart, but that of the whole family.

We built our simple dams with the help of branches of trees growing in the area. These were cut and placed across the stream. The dam was made strong with the help of thick clay we collected along the banks of the streams.

Emptying the section of the stream between the two dams was quite a difficult task. It did not involve only the adults but also children big enough to do so. We took our positions a few steps away from the downstream part of the two dams. With the help of plastic and aluminium basins, trays, pieces of dishware, etc., and working together as a team, we went about our task. Usually it took several hours of hard, backbreaking work under the scorching African sun to achieve our goal.

Our effort was not always rewarded, however! Indeed, on a few occasions we would spend hours empting the demarcated section of the stream only to discover at the end of the day that hardly any fish dwelt there!

It was not always an exercise without reward, however. There were indeed times when Heaven smiled on our endeavour, when our toil was rewarded with a fairly large harvest of fish. On such occasions we returned home all smiles and prepared delicious meals with various tilapia, eels, crabs, etc., which we had harvested.

-22-
WILD HONEY FOR BREAKFAST

ON CERTAIN OCCASIONS we accompanied father to collect honey from bees' nests in the wild. Several weeks or months prior to that, he had discovered a nest in a hollow of a tree that was still standing, or that had fallen. Thereafter he visited it on a regular basis to ascertain the progress of the 'busy bees'.

Finally a time came when he decided enough honeycombs had been established in the wild beehive to warrant their collection. The venture was carried out under the cover of darkness. If he allowed his children to accompany him, he asked them to wait at a safe distance from the nest.

He usually torched the nest with a flame burning from a bundle made from the dry palm branches. That permitted him to destroy most of the bees from a safe distance before he attempted to pick out the combs as quickly as possible. Still some of the bees managed to punish him for attempting to reap where he had not planted! Fortunately, he was not allergic to their stings so, apart from some pain he had to endure for a while, they could not seriously threaten his life.

Back home, we helped father to squeeze the honey out of the honeycombs. The honey so won was preserved in bottles. They were usually kept for home consumption, for what we obtained on such ventures rarely added up to any considerable amount.

-23-
OUR FRIEND BY NIGHT

THE SUN WAS OUR FRIEND during the daytime, whilst the moon was our companion at night, at least during the time it appeared brightly in the skies above our village.

On moonlight nights the children and teenagers of Mpintimpi took advantage of the 'natural electricity' and came out onto the street to play various kinds of games.

One of the games we played on such nights was *Antoakyire*, which means literally 'it was not put behind you'. Though played mainly by boys, it can also be played by both boys and girls together. We all sat in a circle. One of us carrying a piece of cloth tied into a small knot ran behind the circle while at the same time singing:

anto akyire o anto akyire o
anto akyire o anto akyire o
obiba bewu o

At the end of each line, the other players responded in a chorus:

Yom yom yom!

The song was repeated as long as the player continued to run around the group—they could do as many rounds as they chose. The rule of the game forbade those sitting in the circle from turning to look back.

As the player ran, at one stage they dropped the cloth quietly behind one of the seated players and continued running. The person who had the cloth dropped behind them had somehow to get to know what had happened, stand up and chase the first player.

If that did not happen and the runner returned to meet them still seated, the runner gave them a slight touch on the back. The seated player had at that stage to pick up the cloth and make the run. Their place was then taken by the first player. The game continued for a while until the majority decided enough was enough!

Another game that was played on such nights was *Ampe*. *Ampe* is a game played only by girls. It can be played either by just two girls playing alone or two teams of girls. The two players or teams are named as *Ohyiwa* and *Opare*.

During the game, the two players facing each other begin to clap their hands while singing and jumping. As they land, each manipulates her legs, placing one leg forward. *Ohyiwa* wins a point if the left leg meets the other player's right leg, or vice versa. *Oware* wins if the left leg meets the other player's left leg, or if their right legs meet. The first player or team to score ten points wins.

-24-
"SOME ARE COMFORTABLY SEATED WHILE OTHERS ARE SUFFERING IN THEIR SEATS"

O N SOME NIGHTS when the moon shone brightly in the sky, we gathered together to tell *Anansesem* stories. *Anansesem* is a group of Twi fables that involves *Ananse*—a Twi word for spider.

In such fables the spider appears sometimes as a cunning creature that attempts to hide the wisdom of all his fellow creatures in a pot so as to be able to dupe them in the end.

On other occasions *Ananse* is displayed as a mischievous being who seeks to play all sorts of tricks on his fellow human beings to get at their property. *Ananse* could also be kind-hearted, caring for orphans, widows as well as the poor and the neglected.

At this stage, I would like to present to you one of my favourite *Anansesem (Ananse* story). It is entitled *Ebi te yie, ebi nso nte yie koraa.* Translated into English, the title means: 'Some are well and comfortably seated, while others are suffering in their seats.'

As the story goes, there came a point in time when all the members of the Animal Kingdom gathered for a meeting to talk about some of the important matters affecting them. In particular they wanted to talk about the best way to deal with human beings. They considered the human beings selfish and aggressive.

Good luck did not favour Mr Antelope that day. Why not? The answer is that he was given a seat next to Mr Tiger!

Not long after the start of the meeting, Mr Tiger began without any reason to insult and threaten Mr Antelope. Still, Mr Antelope kept quiet. Mr Tiger would not leave matters there. Instead, he began to hit Mr Antelope on the body and also step on his feet.

At one time Mr Antelope wanted to raise his paw to be allowed to speak his mind about the topic being discussed. But no! Mr Tiger would not permit him to do so. He looked angrily into the eyes of Mr Antelope and told him to put his paws down immediately. If he failed to do so he was going to kill him instantly—Mr Tiger made that quite clear.

Soon poor Mr Antelope could bear the suffering no longer. In one brave effort to free himself, he sprang to his feet and cried at the top of his voice: "Attention please, honourable chairperson! I wish to call for the meeting to be postponed immediately!"

"Why?" the chairperson asked.

"Well", Mr Antelope explained nervously, "unfortunately the seating arrangement does not favour everyone; whereas some clearly feel comfortable in their seats, others like myself have been suffering in ours right from the beginning of the meeting!"

The chairperson asked all those who supported the idea of Mr Antelope to raise their paws. Everyone present apart from Mr Tiger did so. Indeed, all of them had noticed what Mr Tiger was doing to Mr Antelope. So the meeting was immediately brought to an end. Mr Antelope immediately fled to his home.

-25-
THE VILLAGE NEWS BROADCASTER AND THE NAUGHTY CHILDREN

THE 'GONG-GONG BEATER' had the duty of announcing to the community any important news or event they needed to know about. He was selected by the Chief from one of the young men of the community.

How does the gong-gong beater go about his job in Mpintimpi? He does so along the main road, that, as I mentioned earlier, divides the little settlement into two almost equal halves. Beginning from one end of the road, he moves towards the other end spreading his message.

Kon-kon; kon-kon; kon-kon, he beats hard on his gong.

"M-p-i-n-t-i-m-p-i-f-o-e!!" he screams at the top of his voice. "I extend warm greetings from Nana. He has asked me to pass such-and-such messages on to you!" Kon-kon; kon-kon—he beats his gong again to signify the end of the announcement.

He then moves on. After a distance of about fifty metres he stops, beats his gong once again and repeats the message. From there he walks another fifty or so metres and repeats the ritual. And so, on and on he goes, moving along the streets of the settlement, beating his gong and broadcasting the message of the Chief to the ears of everyone in every corner of the community.

It was one of the favourite pastimes of my peers, and mine too, to follow the gong-beater as he went about his duty. Children, children! On some occasions, we did not keep silent as we did so, but instead yelled and cried out at the top of our voices, repeating what he had just announced to the community. The community announcer would then turn to us and plead with us to behave decently.

For a short while, we obeyed him and comported ourselves in an orderly fashion. Soon, however, one or more of us began to scream and shout aloud.

At that stage he would turn to chase us away. Whoever was first to be caught could expect a knock on the head, even though they might be innocent!

-26-
A CURIOUS BOXING MATCH ON THE STREETS OF MPINTIMPI

T O EDUCATE THE POPULATION, especially those in the villages, on how to prevent diseases, on the right type of healthy food to eat, the harm that smoking cigarettes causes to our body, etc., the Government sent people specially trained for the job to travel round the country. They travelled in vans. These vans could be described as mobile cinemas, for they showed films wherever they went. The films were mostly about the topics they talked about. In order to draw many people to their meeting, they usually ended the event by showing an exciting film!

Due to the large area they covered, the mobile cinemas visited us once in a blue moon. Usually, the Chief was given a few days' notice before the event. He in turn sent the gong-gong man to inform us about the coming visit.

You can imagine our joy on hearing the news! All of a sudden, the coming visit became 'headline news' everywhere in the village. At school during lessons, the thought of the visit of the mobile cinema occupied my mind even during lessons.

When the day finally arrived, my prayer was that it would not rain in the evening.

Sometimes my prayer was not heard and it rained! At times the rain did not stop until late in the night or even early the next morning. When that happened, the event was usually put off until the next evening.

On one of their visits they showed a film of a fight between our national boxing hero, Floyd Robertson, and Sugar Ramos, a citizen of Cuba. The actual fight had taken place in Accra, our national capital, a few years before. Although the judges declared Sugar Ramos the winner, the supporters and fans of Floyd Robertson, who, as I just mentioned, was from Ghana, thought it was their local hero who had indeed won the fight.

For the next several months, the mobile cinema team took advantage of the interest the people of Ghana had in the fight and showed a film of the match wherever they went.

At last, it was the turn of the inhabitants of Mpintimpi to watch the film on the Floyd Robertson versus Sugar Ramos fight. Those were exciting moments, I tell you.

As if the boxing thriller we had watched was not enough, just as we were about to leave for our homes, I soon noticed from where I was standing someone throwing his fist into the air as if that person was in a fight similar to the one we had just witnessed. Those around him began to run from him.

What was going on? Soon the reason became clear. It involved Kofi Adu, one of my cousins. He was about seven years old at the time. He had fallen asleep during the show and, when his mother awoke him at the end of the show, he began all of sudden to throw punches into the air, in the process hitting anyone who happened to be near him. As he did so, he kept screaming at the top of his voice: "Damn you,

Sugar Ramos, I will teach you a lesson tonight! Yes, I will show you where power lies!"

"Stop it, stop it, Kofi!" his mother called out, trying to calm him, "You are not in a fight with anyone!"

My cousin wouldn't listen and continued for a while to give all around him a 'sound beating'. It took a while for him to return to the real world—indeed, for him to realise he was not Floyd Robertson, and not engaged in a fight with Sugar Ramos.

From that day onwards, Kofi Adu's name became connected with the 'Government cinema'.

-27-
A WELCOME CHANGE TO A DULL VILLAGE LIFE

APART FROM THE MOBILE CINEMA SHOWS, another event that brought some change to the usually dull evening routine of our little settlement was the arrival of the roaming freelance evangelists. With their Bibles in their bags, the evangelists travelled around the country to preach the gospel.

Their coming was not usually announced days ahead; instead, they usually arrived in the morning of the very night they intended to preach. The first port of call on their arrival was as usual the palace. After they had informed the Chief what they were there for, he instructed the gong-gong beater to pass the message on to the community.

Was it because of the change it brought to the somewhat boring nightlife of the village? Was it because of real interest in the message they carried? Whatever the reason, the event was usually well attended.

The meeting began with prayer followed by the singing of a few songs. Sometimes some of the evangelists took time to teach us songs that were not familiar to us to enable us to sing along with them. This was followed by readings from the Bible, and then the actual preaching of the main message of the evening. The session usually lasted for about two hours.

Before we left for our various homes, an offertory was taken to support the work of the roving evangelists.

-28-
THE DRIVERS' ASSISTANTS AND THE CHEEKY VILLAGE BOYS

AT THE TIME I was growing up at Mpintimpi, the transport system in our area was not good enough.

For example, a journey between Mpintimpi and Amantia, mother's home village, a distance of seventy kilometres, could take us almost the whole day! One might wonder why we needed that long for such a short distance?

Firstly, the condition of the roads we travelled on was poor, to say the least.

Secondly, the vehicles we travelled on stopped at almost every village, be it large or small, along our route to allow passengers to get down and new ones to climb on board.

Whenever we decided to visit Amantia, we woke up early in the morning to get ready in time hopefully to catch one of the few vehicles that was travelling in that direction.

Sometimes luck was not on our side and we failed to find a place in any of the vehicles that passed by. We had to wait until the next day to try again.

At other times, there weren't enough empty seats available to take us all. We often travelled in a group, which meant that when a vehicle came by some of us filled the vacant seats while the rest of the group waited for the next vehicle in the hope that there would be more seats available for them.

We had to travel first to Akim Ofoase, a distance of about sixty kilometres. Amantia did not lie on the main road but rather on a less travelled road that joined the main road at Ofoase. It is about seven kilometres away from Ofoase.

When we reached Ofoase, we usually had to wait hours on end for a vehicle to take us to our final goal, Amantia. While the condition of the road from Mpintimpi to Ofoase was poor, the situation was even worse regarding the road leading from Ofoase to Amantia.

In the rainy season, the condition of the road worsened even further. At such times potholes filled with ponds of water that formed in several places on the road. Vehicles that travelled on them risked getting stuck in the middle of the road. When that happened, the passengers joined the driver and his assistant or assistants to try to use human power to free the vehicle from the mud. Sometimes they failed to in their attempt.

When that happened, the passengers were left behind with the vehicle whilst the driver and his assistant or assistants left on foot for the nearest town in search of a tractor to pull the vehicle from the mud. Those whose destinations were not far away usually chose to complete the rest of the journey on foot, carrying their luggage on their heads and/or on their shoulders. Others, who had several kilometres ahead of them, might decide to walk to the next town to seek some shelter and rest until they were able to resume the journey.

As I mentioned earlier, the vehicles that passed through Mpintimpi were usually filled with passengers and goods, often beyond what was officially allowed.

One of the favourite pastimes of my friends and I was to run after such vehicles as they 'crawled' through the village, and scream at the top of our voices: "Sardine! Sardine! Sardine!" As you may have observed, canned sardines on sale at the grocery shop or shopping mall are packed tightly in the cans containing them. By shouting "Sardine! Sardine! Sardine!" we were also drawing attention to the fact that the passengers were tightly packed in the vehicles transporting them.

Such insolence on our part often met with an angry reaction from some of the drivers and their assistants. Some of them, annoyed by our cries, pulled their vehicles to a stop and sent their assistants to chase us. On seeing that, we ran away as fast as our legs could carry us! Some of the assistants would not give up and relentlessly continued to pursue us.

Of course, we had an advantage over them! We lived in the village and knew where to run to, or where to hide. Often we vanished from sight before they could reach us.

We were not always lucky, however. Sometimes we were caught by those chasing us. When that happened they gave us some blows to the body or knocks to the head or both.

-29-
THE COMING OF THE HEALTH INSPECTORS

"CHILDREN, HURRY UP!** Get everything clean and in order, the *Tankase* has just arrived!" Full of excitement on hearing the news, everyone in the house went into action. One of us went to check on the large water barrel we used to collect rainwater that drained from the roof over the main building of our home.

Another went to inspect the large clay pot in the kitchen that served as a reservoir for drinking water.

Yet another one of us went to inspect the small chicken coop at one end of our compound. The remainder of us went round the compound just to make sure everything was tidy and in order.

The coming of the *Tankase* was indeed a cause for commotion in our little village!

You may want to know what *Tankase* stands for, and also what kind of work they were doing.

They were health inspectors sent by the Town Council to go round homes in the community to check that every home and the compound around it was clean. Many of the people who lived in the village could not read or write. So instead of calling the inspectors agents of the Town Council, they just called them *Tankase.*

The inspector who was in charge of Mpintimpi lived at Afosu, a town about five kilometres to the south of our little village. Every four to six weeks he came to do his inspection at our village. We did not know exactly when he would be arriving, however.

In the course of time some of us at home made it a pastime to create false alarms about his supposed coming. When that person returned home from the centre of the village, they would begin in all seriousness:

"Get ready, everyone! The *Tankase* is in town!"

"Are you sure?"

"Sure, sure, sure!"

Soon it was action stations for everyone! To make us think they were telling the truth, that person joined the rest of the family in the general clean-up. After several minutes had passed without any sign of the health inspector, one or the others at home would become suspicious and challenge the informer: "Are you sure he is in town?"

"Maybe he has returned to where he came from!" the pretender would reply jokingly.

"That is not funny!" mother would burst out on hearing this.

Though they appeared to be a source of annoyance to us, a fact that led us to dislike them, the *Tankase* played a very important role in society. They helped us to maintain basic standards of hygiene at home and in so doing helped to prevent the spread of diseases.

-30-
ABANDONED WHEEL RIMS
AS CHURCH BELLS

AT THE TIME I was growing up at Mpintimpi, there were two churches in the village: the Presbyterian as well as the Apostolic Church, the Presbyterian Church being the larger of the two in terms of the average Sunday attendance.

I still remember the church bell of the Presbyterian Church. It was not the type of church bell one would usually associate with a church. The main part of the bell was the metal rim of the wheel of an abandoned vehicle. With the help of a metal chain, the rim was hung on a supporting wooden structure that rose to about a metre above the ground. It stood about fifty metres away from the church building. The bell was sounded with the help of a piece of iron rod, about twenty centimetres long.

Later, when a primary school was built in the village, it also served as the bell that signalled the beginning of the school day.

Although anyone in the church could be called upon to sound the bell, the duty was usually handed to one particular teenage boy at a time.

The Sunday worship service of the Presbyterian Church, 'Presby' for short, began at 10 a.m. The first bell sounded at 8 a.m., to be followed an hour later by the second. In each case, it lasted for about five minutes.

Papa Teacher, the pastor of the Presby Church, was particularly punctual. He usually left home at 9:45 a.m. for the walk to the church. He needed about five minutes to do so. Shortly before he left, he sent someone to instruct the 'bell boy' to sound the third and last bell. At the sound of the third bell, whoever wanted to be in church that morning had to hurry, for Papa Teacher disliked it when worshippers turned up late to disturb the proceedings.

It was a common practice for churches in Ghana to organise a once yearly Harvest and Fundraising Day Service to raise additional funds to support their activities. The little Presbyterian Church at Mpintimpi was no exception. Several weeks before the event, they sent out envelopes to every household in the community and also the surrounding villages—Christian or non-Christian, everyone was called upon to donate money to support God's work.

On Harvest and Fundraising Day, members of the congregation carried various items to church, usually the best produce from their farms or livestock—yams, plantains, pineapples, oranges, hen eggs, etc. The service was attended not only by members of the congregation, but by the community at large. Usually, a well-to-do member of the community was invited to chair the function. The items donated by members were sold and the proceeds kept in the coffers of the church to support its activities.

Looking back, I can only wonder how far the poor peasants were prepared to go in terms of financial sacrifice to ensure the smooth running of their church.

The Presby Church had a singing band, a kind of choir. On occasions such as Christmas and Easter, they made a procession through the main street of the village and filled the atmosphere with inspiring gospel songs.

-31-
CHRISTMAS CAROLS FOR BISCUITS

A T THE TIME I WAS GROWING UP in little Mpintimpi, Christmas was generally referred to as 'a festival for children'. This was because it was usually at that time of the year that many parents managed to afford to purchase new clothes for their children. By chance, Christmas falls about the same time as the major cocoa-harvesting season. This placed many parents in a position to present their children with new clothes to celebrate the occasion.

The term 'new clothes' could be misleading. It could for example lead the stranger to our environment to imagine it referred to items like a shirt of the best brand, a designer coat, a cute pair of trousers, an admirable pair of shoes of the best brand, etc. This was not the case, for our parents could not afford luxuries. We had instead to content ourselves with pieces of cotton clothing known locally as *ntama*, which I referred to earlier on. Each child in our little village usually received a piece of *ntama* to mark the occasion. Shoes to accompany the piece of clothing were out of the question.

The day after Christmas, the 26th December, also known as Boxing Day, was a special day for the children of Mpintimpi, for it was on that day we received our long-awaited new *ntama*. A stranger to the village, at least on the 26th of December, would have little difficulty figuring out which of the several children that assembled on the streets shared the same parents, for it was the practice of parents to present their children with the same type of *ntama* for the occasion.

If only for the sake of being seen, almost every child in the village attended church that day. After service we went in small groups from house to house singing Christmas carols. In return we were usually given biscuits.

Christmas also offered us the opportunity to enjoy rich meals cooked with rice, chicken, mutton and beef, something we could only dream of on an ordinary day.

It is customary to share food prepared at Christmas with relatives, friends and neighbours. They are not invited home; instead, they are sent portions of the meal in small bowls and dishes. The duty fell on the children to carry out such deliveries.

Mother was especially kind-hearted. Particularly at Christmas, she sought to share our meal with as many as possible. The result was that we were often left with little meat for ourselves. We had waited all year long for the opportunity to enjoy our delicacies, only to feel short-changed when the time finally arrived!

-32-
POCKET MONEY EARNED
THE HARD WAY

I **DID NOT RECEIVE ANY POCKET MONEY** from our parents; the same could be said of every child growing up in our community.

When we were big enough to do so, we found means by which we could earn some money for ourselves. One important avenue open to us was through the sale of kola nuts. Apart from growing cocoa, a few residents of the village reserved part of their land for the cultivation of kola nut trees.

The kola nut tree, which grows well in tropical climates, can attain a height of about twenty metres. It bears fruits that can contain several nuts which have a bitter taste.

Chewing kola nuts is not popular with the population of southern Ghana. The situation is different among the tribes in the north of the country as well as other inhabitants of the west African sub-region, in particular Nigeria.

There is something about the kola tree that is not found with the cocoa tree. The cocoa fruit, also known as pods, when ripe, will remain on the tree or its branches, as the case may be, until it is harvested. It goes rotten on the tree if that does not happen. The situation is different with the kola fruit. If it is left unharvested for a while after reaching maturity it falls to the ground. The rain and also wind favour this process.

The children in the village, and to some extent some adults, took advantage of this and got up early in the morning and visited the various kola farms in and around the village looking for fruits that might have fallen down during the night.

"That amounted to reaping where you had not sown!" you might point out. While not disagreeing with you, I would like to explain that our society did not consider it an offence to do so. Usually the farmers waited for the most favourable time, a time when several fruits had all together reached maturity, to harvest their crop. Hardly any of them were prepared to visit their farms on a daily basis to look for fruits that had dropped down overnight.

What we were not permitted to do was to actively pluck the fruits ourselves. Whoever was caught by a landowner doing so had to face the penalties of that unaccepted behaviour.

If it involved a child or a teenager, the landowner might decide to punish the person on the spot. In that case, the landowner would probably cut a stalk from the bush and give them a dose of whipping! If, on the other hand, the offender was an adult, the owner might decide to bring the case before other elderly members of the village to seek settlement.

The kola nuts were sold to traders who bought them to sell in the northern part of the country as well as Nigeria and other parts of west Africa. Usually they were sold in quantities of hundreds; the price for a hundred kola nuts was not always the same—it went up and down, depending on the time of year and also whether the harvest was abundant or lean.

Another way we earned pocket money was to perform various kinds of odd jobs. One of the common ones involved clearing cocoa farms of weeds before the cocoa pods were harvested. From the point of view of the person who has no idea of cocoa farming this may appear to be a job too difficult for teenagers to do. I must say that weeding under mature cocoa trees is not very difficult. Usually the leaves of mature cocoa trees form a canopy, something like an umbrella, that prevents direct sunlight from reaching the ground below them. Since plants require sufficient sunlight to grow, many of them are not able to grow under the canopy formed by the cocoa trees, making it easy, even for children of our age, to clear them.

We usually performed such jobs during the holidays, either on days when our parents were engaged in communal labour—sometimes the whole adult population met to work for the good of the whole village; this type of work was known as communal labour—or when an event such as a funeral celebration prevented us from working on our own farms.

One could also be asked to clear the weeds growing in someone's back yard in exchange for some money.

At other times my peers and I went on an expedition to hunt animals such as squirrels, Gambian pouched rats, grasscutters, etc. Sometimes we returned from a whole day's expedition empty-handed. At other times fortune smiled on us, and we returned with our hunting sack filled with various kinds of game. On such occasions, we gave part of our catch to our parents and sold the rest. The money we obtained was shared equally among ourselves.

-33-
ORANGES AS FOOTBALL

FOOTBALL is the most popular sport in Ghana. The situation was no different at the time I was growing up. Whenever our time allowed us, my friends and I got together to play football. We made use of any large open space we could find. In most cases we did not play with proper balls because we did not have them. Instead, we played with oranges!

Whenever one of us wanted to play football, he went round from house to house and asked his friends to join him. After he had found enough friends wanting to play, they went round inspecting the orange trees growing in and around the village for an orange fruit big enough for the purpose.

Sometimes some of our relatives living in the large towns paid a visit to the village and presented us with a plastic ball. You can imagine our joy on those occasions! When we were lucky, we could play with the plastic balls for many weeks, sometimes even many months before they got torn apart.

There were times when we were not lucky, when the new balls got punctured by a sharp object such as a piece of broken glass, a needle or the thorn of a plant growing along the edges of the playground. When that happened we were left with no choice but to return to our oranges and hope for a time in the future when someone might present us with yet another proper ball.

-34-
THE YOUNG TRAVELLER WHO MISSED HIS MOTHER'S KITCHEN

AS I MENTIONED at the beginning of my narration, at the time I was big enough to attend school there was no school in our little village. Four years after starting school the local authorities decided to open a primary school in our little village. It was too late for us because it only started with Year 1 pupils. At that time I was already starting my Year 5.

Teacher Ansah was one of the first teachers of the school. He did not come from Mpintimpi. Instead he came from a town called Twereso, which is about eighty kilometres from Mpintimpi. The whole village welcomed him warmly into their midst.

Teacher Ansah rented a room in father's extended family home. Father and mother showed him kindness, treating him as one of their children.

In the course of time I became his best friend in the village. I cannot explain why he chose me as his friend. I was not attending his school. Besides that, there were several other kids in the village he could have befriended.

One evening, a few days before schools closed for the Christmas holiday, he approached father and said:

"I would like to take my little friend along with me for the Christmas holidays!"

"Really?" father replied, rather surprised.

"Yes! I would like to show him to my parents and the rest of the family."

"I do not have anything against it. I will pass the message on to his mother and himself to know what they think about the idea."

Mother was not very sure whether I would be able to leave home for a while without missing my parents and my siblings. When she saw how happy I was about the idea, she agreed with father to allow me to travel with my friend.

I could hardly wait for the day to arrive. There were two reasons why I was delighted about the journey with my friend. In the first place the idea of travelling on a vehicle was attractive. I rarely had the chance to do so before. Once in a while mother took us on a visit to her hometown Amantia, but those were very rare indeed. There were some other few occasions when drivers of vehicles stopped and gave us a lift to or from school.

Also, this new chance to explore an unknown place was attractive.

The awaited day finally arrived! Together with my big friend we boarded a vehicle that took us safely to our destination. I was warmly welcomed by his family. Soon I was mingling with the family members of my age group. On the street, they introduced me to their peers, who in turn greeted me warmly, extending the invitation to me to join them in a game of football whenever I could.

Mother was right when she thought I would feel homesick, however. A few days after the arrival of the 'village boy' in town, I indeed began to feel homesick! Not that I was not accepted by my hosts. No, they were really nice to me. It was something else that led to my problem—my stomach!

At home there was always plenty of food—plantain, yam, cocoyam, cassava, maize, etc. At Mpintimpi, latest by eight in the morning, the first meal of the day—boiled plantain to go with *nkotomire* (leaves from the cocoyam plant) stew— was ready. It was followed about four hours later, most likely, with more boiled plantain and sauce made from garden eggs (vegetables found in Ghana). Not long thereafter mother set about to prepare *fufu*.

The situation was very different when compared to the meals provided by my hosts. Usually we had to wait till late in the morning—towards midday, in fact, to eat the first meal of the day!

Nothing usually followed thereafter until the evening meal. Not only that, the quantity of food served was not sufficient for me.

At Mpintimpi, our farm was not far away from the village. It was different with my friend's family, and we had to walk a long distance to visit the farmland.

At the beginning I tried to be brave. Soon I could no longer hide my tears. Some members of the household who saw me crying reported the matter to my big friend.

At first he tried to cheer me up.

"Don't worry, we have only a few days left", he told me.

Still, I could not keep my tears back. I just longed to be back home.

In the end, my big friend had no choice but to cut short our visit and return to Mpintimpi. You can imagine the joy in my eyes when I stepped back onto the soil of my beloved village!

-35-
THE VILLAGE BOY
GOES TO TOWN

AT THE BEGINNING OF 1971, I applied to sit the common entrance examination. A pass in it was required for admission to a secondary school. Admission to a secondary school opened the door to several chances for further education. From the secondary school one could go on to university.

Those who were not able to go to the secondary school completed the ten-year elementary education with the Standard Seven Certificate. It was also known as the Middle School Leaving Certificate.

Usually it was only the children of the rich who were able to attend the secondary school. The reason is that many of the secondary schools were boarding schools. Unfortunately the farmers and the ordinary workers were not able to afford the boarding fees.

To help the children of the poor farmers to attend the secondary school, the CMB which stands for Cocoa Marketing Board put some money aside to help pay for the fees of children of cocoa farmers who did very well at school.

Although my parents were poor, I was able to attend a secondary school. At the beginning my elder brother who was working paid my fees. Later I received financial assistance from the CMB.

On Thursday 16th September 1971, I joined a vehicle filled almost to the last seat that was heading for Akim Oda, the capital town of our district. I was on my way to attend the Oda Secondary School.

Moving from Mpintimpi to the boarding school was like moving from the middle of the jungle into a modern city. All of a sudden, I was privileged to enjoy the luxury of living with electricity and all the other facilities associated with it—electric fans to cool our classrooms and dormitories, TV, electric irons, etc.

From that day, I would no longer walk without wearing shoes or a pair of sandals. Even if I wanted to do so, the rules of the boarding school would not permit it.

At Mpintimpi I used chewing sticks such as *tweapea* and *nsorkodua* to clean my teeth. This changed when I got to the boarding school. Over there every student was expected to use a toothbrush and toothpaste.

Also, I was no longer permitted to eat with my fingers. Three times every day, morning, afternoon and evening, the whole school gathered in a large hall, the dining hall, for meals. Every student was expected to eat with a set of cutlery.

You may wonder how someone like me who had never used a set of cutlery in my life was able to use them! Well, our teachers asked those who knew how to do so to teach those who didn't.

Our friends taunted us, by calling us *nhabanmamu fo*. In the Twi language *nhabanmamu fo* means 'those who come from the bush'!

Every Sunday evening there was a church service. Each student had to put on a pair of white trousers, a white shirt, a tie and a white coat. I and the other *nhabanmamu fo* did not know how to put on a tie! In this case also our classmates from the towns and cities helped us.

After almost twelve weeks' stay, I returned to Mpintimpi for the Christmas holidays. My stay had taught me several new things but had not changed me. Though life would not be the same as before, I still accompanied my parents to the farm and enjoyed the company of my family and friends I left behind in the village.

EPILOGUE
GHANA 2, USA 1

T HE STORY YOU HAVE READ happened about forty years ago. You may want to know if things have changed in my little village.

If you are person who loves football, or soccer, as it is also called, you may remember that when the 2010 Football World Cup was played in South Africa, Ghana beat the USA 2–1.

The next day I called Manu, my sister at Mpintimpi! Yes indeed, today, thanks to the introduction of the mobile phone, I can talk to her even from Europe. (As might be expected, there is no proper telephone in the village.)

"We are still celebrating Ghana's victory over the US", she said. "It was a great game!"

"Did you watch it?"

"Yes, I watched it live on TV."

"You mean you have your own TV?"

"Yes—one of our relatives gave me one recently!"

"Is that the only TV set in the village?"

"No, a few people in the village have their own sets!"
Imagine, being able to watch the World Cup live at Mpintimpi!

My thoughts went back to the Football World Cup Final between Holland and Germany in 1974! On that occasion, my brothers and I had to go round the village looking for a transistor radio so we could follow the commentary. In the end we spotted one and were permitted to hang around to listen as Germany beat Holland 2–1 to lift the World Cup.

Now, almost 36 years later, Mpintimpi seemed to have moved on. But do not be deceived into thinking that things have changed much there. Yes, it's true that now they have electricity. Several years ago the government decided to erect an electricity line to connect two large towns in the area. Because the line passed near the village, the village also profited from it. Still, several of the inhabitants are not able to afford to pay to have electricity brought into their homes. Such individuals still rely on the kerosene lamps I spoke about earlier on—yes, the lamps that helped me do my homework!

Nevertheless, one can still say that compared to the situation that existed in my childhood days, there has been some improvement in the living conditions of the inhabitants of the little village of Mpintimpi.

www.ingramcontent.com/pod-product-compliance
Lightning Source LLC
Chambersburg PA
CBHW060123050426

42448CB00010B/2006